SCIENCE
THROUGH THE SEASONS

WINTER

GABRIELLE WOOLFITT

Wayland

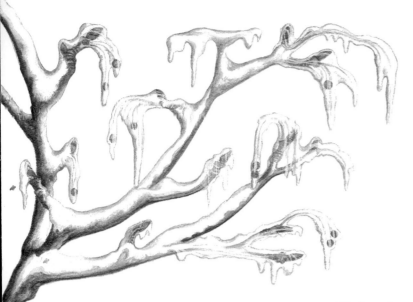

Titles in the series:

Spring
Summer
Autumn
Winter

Series editor: Katie Orchard
Series designer: Pinpoint Design
Artist: Pauline Allen
Production controller: Carol Titchener
Photo stylist: Zoë Hargreaves

First published in 1995 by Wayland (Publishers) Ltd
61 Western Road, Hove, East Sussex, BN3 1JD, England

British Library Cataloguing in Publication Data
Woolfitt, Gabrielle
Winter. – (Science Through the Seasons series)
I. Title II. Series
508

ISBN 0 7502 1461 9

Typeset in Britain by Dorchester Typesetting Group Ltd
Printed and bound by L.E.G.O. S.p.A., Vicenza, Italy

Cover pictures: A dormouse sleeping (far left), some winter twigs (top right) and a snow flake (bottom).

Title page picture: A ewe and lamb feeding on winter food

Contents

Words in **bold** are in the glossary on page 30.

What is Winter?

Winter is the coldest season of the year. The days are short and the nights are long and dark. In winter, the sun is low in the sky. It may even be cold enough to snow. When it is very cold, frost forms on the trees and icicles hang from the roofs.

People dress up warmly at this time of year. Animals need to stay warm too. They often live in **burrows** for the winter. Most plants do not grow in winter because there is not enough sunlight, and many trees lose all their leaves.

Holly ▶

◀ Pear

Mountain ash ▲

▼ Jay

Winter is the end of nature's year. But under the ground, plants are ready to grow when spring comes. Animals get ready to give birth when winter is over.

Oak ▶

Many thousands of years ago, ancient people watched the changing seasons. At Stonehenge in England, they built a circle of stones. At the winter **solstice** the sun sets exactly between these two stones.

Woodpecker ▶

Stoat ▶

◀ Snowdrops

Winter Around the World

Wherever you live in the world, winter is the coldest time of the year. Winter starts on the winter solstice.

In the northern **hemisphere**, winter lasts from December until March. In Australia and South America, which are in the southern hemisphere, winter starts in June and ends in September.

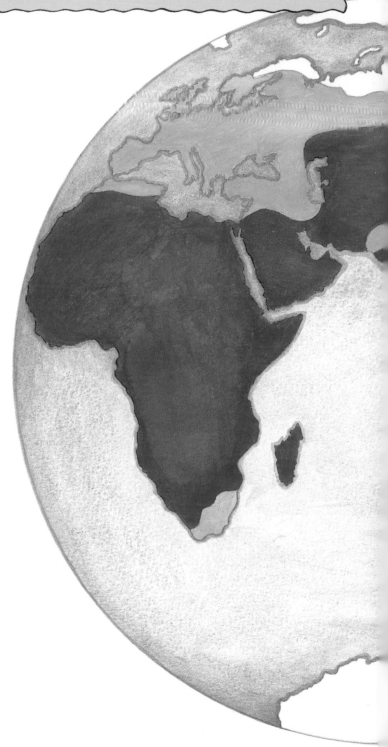

Congwong bay in Sydney, Australia. The winter is not very cold here and most houses do not need central heating.

Northern winter		Always hot	
Southern winter		Always cold	

In Antarctica it is cold all year round.

Most of northern Europe and Canada have a cold winter with snow and ice. The temperature is usually about 0 °C.

Countries near the **equator** have hot weather all year round, and winter is only slightly cooler than summer. If you live near the **Arctic** Circle, winter is very cold and dark. During autumn, the sun gets lower in the sky and the days get shorter, until one day the sun does not rise. Then it is totally dark for a few weeks.

Winter Weather

What is the weather like in winter? It all depends on where you live. In Tunisia, in North Africa, the temperature stays at around 14–18 °C even in the middle of winter. In Siberia, in the north of Russia, the temperature can drop to -40 °C.

◀ Blackthorn

Hawthorn ▶

Mallard ducks ▶

◀ Common hare

Bullrushes ▶

What is winter like where you live? You could look at the weather every day and make a chart to show what you notice. To be **accurate**, you should check the weather at the same time each day.

Day	Temperature
Day 1	3 °C
Day 2	-1 °C
Day 3	6 °C

◄ Ash

Scientists often use symbols on charts and maps so that people all over the world can understand what they mean. Measure the temperature outside when you look at the weather. Record it in a chart and think of a symbol to show that type of weather.

▲ Reeds

Why is Winter Cold?

The Earth is warmed by sunlight. In winter, days are short and cold because there is little sunlight. The sun is also low in the sky. This experiment shows you why winter is cold.

YOU WILL NEED:
a large ball, a narrow beam torch, plain paper, a pencil or crayon.

▲ 1. One person holds the ball up. Another person stands two metres away with the torch.

◀ 2. Point the torch at the centre of the ball. A third person holds the paper against the ball and draws around the spot of light.

The torch shining at the top of the ball is like the low winter sun shining on the Earth. The sunlight and heat spread out so it is cold.

▲ 3. Now aim all the torchlight at the top of the ball. Draw this patch of light on fresh paper. Is this spot of light different from the light in the first test?

▲ 4. Look at the drawings from each test. In which one is the light most spread out?

Hail, Snow and Sleet

When it is warm, water droplets in the clouds fall as rain. In winter, the temperature is often below 0 °C. It is too cold to rain because water freezes at 0 °C. So in winter, the water droplets in clouds freeze before reaching the ground and form **hail** – frozen raindrops. As the rain falls, it gets so cold that it freezes into little balls of ice.

◀ Crows

Pony ▶

▼ Squirrel tracks

Squirrel ▶

◀ Robin

▲ Fox tracks

◀ Holly

Hare tracks ▲

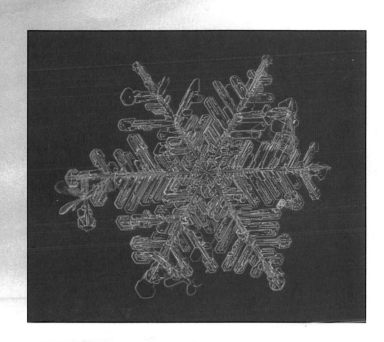

Snow is made of flakes of frozen water. Every snowflake is different. Snowflakes are built into six-pointed stars. If you look at snowflakes with a hand-lens you can see amazing shapes. Snow is light and airy. It floats down to earth and can be blown around in the wind. When snow is packed together it forms ice.

This snowflake has six points. No two snowflakes are the same.

▲ Field mouse

Jackdaw ▶

Sleet is a mixture of snow and rain. It is very cold and wet. Sleet stings your face.

Winter nights are very cold. Ponds and puddles can freeze over. These experiments look at ice.

▲ 2. Mark the level of the water with a marker pen, and put the jar into your freezer.

▼ 3. Leave it for a day. Mark the new level of the ice.

YOU WILL NEED:

a small glass jar or a clear plastic container, water, a marker pen, a glass, a freezer, some ice cubes.

▲ 1. Pour some water into a jar.

Ice takes up more room than water does.

▲ 1. Pour some water into a glass.

2. Put some ice cubes into the water. ▲

▲ 3. Try to push them to the bottom. What happens?

Ice floats on water.

◀ 4. Leave the glass for ten minutes. Where has the ice gone?

Ice melts as it warms up.

Hibernation

Many animals cannot survive the cold winter. Some animals go to sleep in a warm place for the winter. This is called **hibernation**.

Most insects die at the end of autumn. Some insects will hibernate through the winter. They wake up again in the warmer spring weather.

◄ Red squirrel

◄ Beech

◄ Ladybirds

Fallow deer ▼   Scots pine ►

◄ Queen wasp

Hedgehog ▼

Bats ▼

Moth pupa ▲

This dormouse has made a cosy nest in the straw at the edge of a field. It will stay curled up to keep warm until spring comes.

Small animals like mice try to find a warm house or a barn to live in through winter. Dormice make themselves a warm nest in a field and curl up to survive the coldest weather. Although most large animals do not normally hibernate, bears in cold parts of the USA hibernate in caves. **Polar bears** have very special thick coats. They do not need to hibernate.

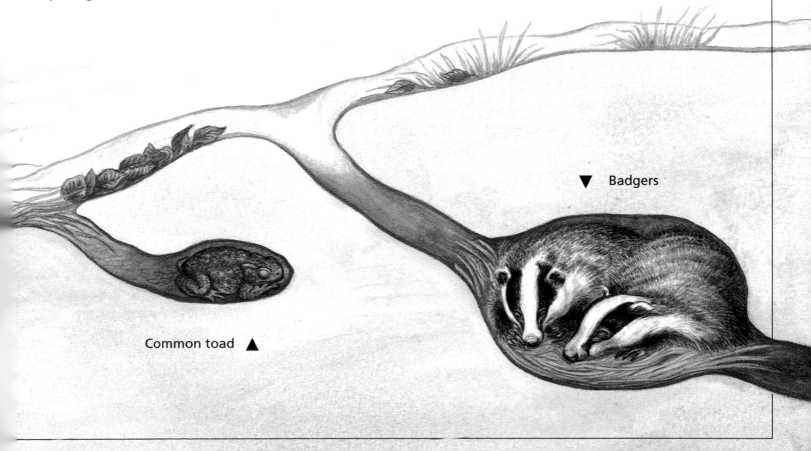

Common toad ▲

▼ Badgers

Small animals get cold faster than big animals. This experiment shows you why small animals need to hibernate and most big animals do not.

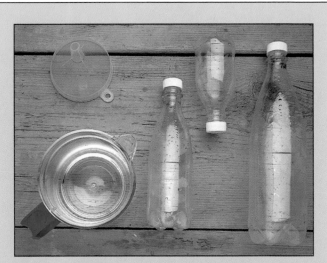

YOU WILL NEED:

three different-sized plastic bottles, a funnel, a jug, warm water, somewhere cold.

▲ 1. Fill each bottle with warm water. Put the tops on tight and put the bottles in a cold place for one hour.

▲ 2. Collect the bottles. Shake each bottle a few times.

◀ 3. Feel the outside of each bottle. Which one feels the coldest? Which one feels the warmest? Is there a more accurate way to measure the temperature?

The small bottle became cold faster than the big bottle. Small animals can freeze to death if they go out when it is too cold.

19

Keeping Warm

Animals and people need to stay warm in winter. This experiment will help you find out about keeping warm.

YOU WILL NEED:

three empty, 1 litre plastic bottles with tops, cotton wool, artificial fur, string, scissors, a funnel, a jug, warm water, a thermometer, paper, a pencil, a cold place.

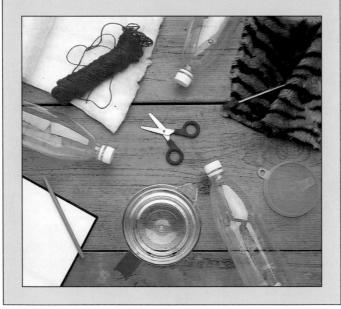

▲ 1. Wrap one bottle in cotton wool, one in artificial fur, and leave one bottle unwrapped.

▲ 2. Pour 1 litre of warm water into a jug. Note its temperature.

The warm water in the bottle is like the warm blood in your body. If you do not wrap up well you will get very cold.

▲ 3. Pour the warm water into each of the bottles and put the lids on. Put all three bottles somewhere cold – a fridge is best.

4. After an hour, collect the bottles. ▶ Measure the temperature of the water in each bottle. Write down the results. Which bottle stayed the warmest?

Birds in Winter

Birds do not hibernate in winter. It is hard for birds to find food in the snow. Some birds **migrate** to warmer countries. You can help to feed the birds that stay behind by making a bird feeder.

YOU WILL NEED:

a plastic bottle, a plant pot stand, a hole-punch, two garden canes, string, bird seed or nuts.

1. Ask an adult to cut the bottom off the bottle and to make four holes, 1 cm from the bottom. Put the sticks through the holes to make a cross. ▶

▲ 2. Balance the sticks on the plant pot stand. Leave a gap between the bottom of the bottle and the base of the plant pot stand.

▲ 3. Thread the string under the plant pot stand and tie it tightly at each end of one of the sticks.

▲ 4. Repeat this with another length of string and the other stick.

▲ 5. Tie a firm double-loop of string around the neck of the bottle. Make a loop to hang the bottle by and fix this to the opposite side of the bottle neck.

▲ 6. Fill the feeder with bird seed or nuts. Hang the feeder outside and see which birds visit.

Winter On the Farm

In winter, the fields may be covered in snow or ice. Most animals will need to be kept indoors. The farmer must give the animals food because they cannot reach the grass.

Most plants will not grow in winter so the farmer uses the time to prepare for the next year. Walls are mended. New gates are put up. The fields are left bare so the freezing cold can break up the soil.

(Right) This sheep is licking the lamb to clean it after its birth.

▼ Winter wheat

◄ Hawthorn

◄ Apple tree

▼ Hedge laying

▼ Fence mending

Sheep stay outside, even when it snows. Lambs are born at the end of winter, sometimes when there is still snow on the ground. The farmer must wrap up the lambs as soon as they are born. The mother **ewes** and their lambs stay in a warm shed until the lambs are old enough to survive the cold.

Elms ▼

Winter feed ▼

Ewe ▶

◀ Lambs

The Night Sky

At night, you can see the stars and the moon because there is no bright sunlight.

Winter is a good time to look at the night sky. It gets dark early in the evening. You can look for stars and the moon before bedtime every night. On a clear night, try to find a dark place away from electric light. Look at the sky. You may see a few stars and the moon. If you look for a while you will see more stars.

You can see the moon move across the sky in this picture. Every night it seems to change shape over a month, and then it disappears. This is because we can only see the part that is lit up by sunlight. As the moon moves around the Earth, different parts are lit up.

(Main picture) The moon changing shape over a month.

These stars make the shape of the giant, Orion. The three bright stars in the middle form his belt.

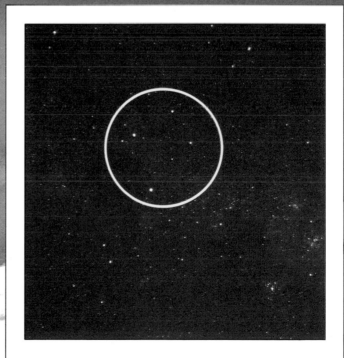

The Southern Cross (in the circle) can be seen in the southern hemisphere. The bottom star points towards the South Pole.

Spring is Coming

When you hear the birds singing in the trees and notice that the sun is rising earlier in the morning, you know that spring is coming.

Under the ground, **bulbs** are getting ready to grow into daffodils and tulips. At the end of winter, some flowers begin to push through the snow. Birds get into pairs and start to build **nests**. Sleepy insects come out from hibernation and start to buzz around the early flowers.

At the end of winter crocuses and snowdrops push their way through the snow. When you see these flowers you know that the weather will soon get warmer.

Ladybird ▶

Hazel ▲

Badger ▶

Bluebells ▲

As the days get longer, the weather gets warmer. You can see lambs in the fields and buds on the trees. Some bushes flower at the end of winter and most trees send out new green leaves. Soon it will be spring.

Maple ▶

Red squirrel ▶

Sheep ▼

▲ Rabbits

Hedgehog ▶

◀ Celandine

Blue tit ▼

▼ Aconite

▼ Blackthorn

▼ Bumble bee

Glossary

accurate   Correct, or exactly right.

Arctic   The cold region of the world around the North Pole.

bulbs   These are onion-shaped, and contain food for certain plants, ready for when they start to grow again in the spring.

burrows   Holes in the ground in which certain animals live.

equator   An imaginary line around the Earth, half-way between the North and South Poles.

ewes   Female sheep.

hail   Small pieces of ice that fall from the sky like rain.

hemisphere   Half of the globe. The two hemispheres are usually called the northern and southern hemispheres.

hibernation   To sleep for a long time during the cold weather. Animals and insects which hibernate wake up in the spring.

migrate   To move to a warmer country in winter.

nests   Homes made by birds, mice and other animals for their young.

polar bears   Very large, white bears that live in the Arctic.

sleet   Partly melted snow or hail.

solstice   The longest day of the year in the northern hemisphere is the summer solstice, which is on 21 June. The shortest day is the winter solstice, on 21 December.

Books to Read

Projects for Winter by Celia McInnes (Wayland, 1989)

Science Activities: Meteorology by Graham Peacock (Wayland, 1994)

Winter in the Wood by Janet Fitzgerald (Evans, 1989)

Winter on the Farm by Janet Fitzgerald (Evans, 1989)

Winter Weather by John Mason (Wayland, 1990)

Picture Acknowledgements

Eye Ubiquitous 25, 28; Science Photo Library 5, 27 (both); Tony Stone *cover* (far left), *back cover* (bottom), 6, 7, 17; Wayland Picture Library *cover* (photograph by Colin S. Milkins) top right, *back cover* (photograph by Colin S. Milkins) top left, *title page*; Zefa *cover* (bottom right).

The commissioned photographs used in this book were taken by APM Studios.

The publishers would like to thank the staff and children at Somerhill School, Hove, Sussex, for their kind assistance.

Index